FROM THE MORNING OF THE WORLD

FROM THE MORNING OF THE WORLD

Poems from the Manyoshu
The first anthology of Japanese poetry

Translated by
Graeme Wilson

HARVILL
An Imprint of HarperCollins*Publishers*

First published in Great Britain 1991 by Harvill
an imprint of HarperCollins Publishers
77/85 Fulham Palace Road
Hammersmith, London W6 8JB

9 8 7 6 5 4 3 2 1

A CIP catalogue record for this book is available from the British Library

ISBN 0–00–271078–1

Typeset by Gloucester Typesetting Services
Bond's Mill, Stonehouse, Gloucestershire
Designed by Libanus Press, Marlborough
Printed and bound in Great Britain by
Hartnolls Ltd, Bodmin, Cornwall

for Robin

Acknowledgements are made to the editors of the following publications in which various of these translations have appeared:

Ariel, Asahi Evening News, Asian & Pacific Quarterly, Asian Culture Quarterly, Bangkok Magazine, Christian Science Monitor, Cornhill Magazine, Dalhousie Review, Denver Quarterly, Encounter, English, Hatbox, Hemisphere, Imago, Jacaranda Review, Japan Quarterly, Listener, Literary Review, Literature in North Queensland, London Magazine, Look East, Nation Review, New Statesman, New York Times, Oriental Economist, Poetry North West, Quadrant, Rhinoceros Magazine, Salt, Solidaridad, Southern Review, Spectator, Sydney Morning Herald, Tablet, Texas Quarterly, Tribune, Twentieth Century, Westerly, Western Humanities Review, Windsor Review, The World & I

CONTENTS

* designates a woman poet

CONTENTS

CONTENTS

THOUGH the *Manyoshu* is relatively little known in the West, it is, in fact, one of the great works of world literature and is still the basis of the teaching of all poetry in Japan. Poetry is fundamental to Japanese culture and the *Manyoshu* is the foundation stone for poetry in Japan, and virtually every living Japanese knows about it and can even quote from it. It ranks in poetic stature with the Chinese *Shi Ching* and the Palatine edition of the *Greek Anthology*. Indeed, no one can count himself truly civilized who is unaware of the poetic trove contained within it.

The *Manyoshu*, which probably but not certainly means the *Myriad Leaves Collection*, is the earliest surviving anthology of poetry in the Japanese language. This somewhat laboured sentence reflects the need for the maximum possible precision in an unavoidably vague situation. Thus, we do not know the actual date of the *Manyoshu*'s composition. Though its last dated poem is from 759, the main work of compilation was probably carried out in the years 744–746 when its chief compiler, Otomo no Yakamochi (718–785) was known to be otherwise unoccupied in the capital city of Nara (then called Hejo). Yakamochi was almost certainly working under the general direction of the then Great Minister, Tachibana no Moroe (684–757) who seems to have been the prime mover in the creation of a collection of Japanese poetry designed to demonstrate that the people of Yamato could match, and even surpass, the Chinese poetry already well known in the cultivated and literary circles of Japan. Yakamochi, the son of Otomo no Tabito (665–731) who was himself a famous poet and court-aristocrat, had already by the mid-740s shown himself to be an up-and-coming poet with all the skills necessary to implement Tachibana's project.

Chinese influences, both by direct contact and particularly

through the intermediary Korean states in which the Japanese upper class had itself originated, had increasingly been affecting all political, religious and cultural developments inside Japan since the early seventh century. Indeed, in the field of poetry, this mainland influence had led to the appearance in 751, several years before Yakamochi ceased work on the compilation of the *Manyoshu*, of an anthology of 120 poems in Chinese written by Japanese courtiers, the *Kaifuso* (*Fond Recollections of Poetry*). Even the *Manyoshu* itself, though essentially an expression of Japaneseness, does contain a handful of poems in Chinese; and the often lengthy head-notes to its poems in Japanese (from which comes much of our information about the anthology, in some cases detailing not only the circumstances but the very day of the poem's composition) are also normally written in Chinese.

As to the *Manyoshu*'s claim to be the earliest surviving collection of poems in Japanese, the anthology itself records that hundreds of its 4516 constituent poems were drawn from such earlier anthologies of Japanese poetry as the *Kokashu* (*Collection of Old Songs*) and from other collections of poems by earlier and near-contemporary writers such as Kakinomoto no Hitomaro, Takahashi no Sakimaro and Kasa Kanamura. All these cited collections are now lost except in so far as some of the poems they included have been preserved in the *Manyoshu*. Even that preservation is extraordinary, resulting from the political fluke that all Yakamochi's papers were confiscated into the archives of the central government when, within days of his death, his nephew was involved in an unsuccessful conspiracy and the whole Otomo clan fell into political disgrace and a virtual extinction from which the already-established power and still-growing influence of the Fujiwara family ensured that it never really recovered. The bureaucrats running the Chinese-style administration introduced by the Emperor Temmu (622–686) took over that control earlier exercised by warriors of the Otomo type, and from the mid-eighth to the twelfth centuries Japan would remain under Fujiwara influence. 'I do believe,' said Fujiwara no Michinaga in 1017 when another of his daughters married an Emperor, 'that this whole world is mine.' And so indeed it had become.

These many uncertainties about the origin of the *Manyoshu* are further complicated by the fact that, until the later invention of two Japanese scripts, *katakana* by Kibi no Makibi (693–775) and *hirogana* by Kobo Daishi (774–835), there were no means of writing the Japanese language. To cope with this situation, official records were kept in Chinese while a rudimentary phonetic script (*manyogana*, so named after its use in recording the poems in the *Manyoshu*) was employed to record the sounds of Japanese words using Chinese symbols having the same sounds (but usually different meanings) in spoken Chinese. This phoneticism was made more difficult to interpret by an admixture of Chinese symbols used purely for their semantic content. Consequently, it is not surprising that certain irreverent critics have argued that substantial numbers of the poems in the *Manyoshu* can be juggled to mean whatever any particular interpreter would like them to mean; and scholarly debate as to the precise meaning of such poems has continued to the present day since the Priest Sengaku (1203–1273) produced the first major critical study of the *Manyohus* in his ten-volume *Sengaku Soranjo* in the mid-thirteenth century. Earlier attempts to decipher the texts, such as that upon which Minamoto no Shitago (911–983) had embarked in 951 at Imperial command, had achieved nothing substantial. A further complicating consideration in deciphering *manyogana* derives from the totally different word orders and grammatical structures in Chinese and Japanese, with the consequent requirement in *manyogana* for diacritical marks beside the Chinese symbols (to indicate, amongst other things, the correct word order). Errors, omissions and losses in the copying of the earliest (now lost) written texts of the *Man-yoshu* thus provided generous scope for distortion of the original poets' poetic intentions. In as much as any translator must expect criticism of the literal accuracy of his work, the translator of the *Manyoshu* is unusually well armoured. Not even the most scholarly critic can be sure that his own particular understanding of the *Manyoshu* is in fact correct; and I personally believe (very much in the general Japanese tradition) that in this specific field the heart (*kokoro*) is a better guide than even those heads most heavily laden with academic laurels. It is here perhaps worth nothing that the Koreans, who could not write their own language until *hangul* was invented by a committee of scholars in 1446, were similarly obliged to use Chinese symbols to construct the so-called *idu* script used to record early material in the Korean language.

★ ★ ★

The compilation of the *Manyoshu* almost certainly originated in a desire of the Japanese court to demonstrate that Yamato had already produced and was still producing poetry of a quality at least as good as the Chinese poetry familiar to its courtiers from such huge Chinese anthologies as the sixth-century 30-volume *Wen Hsuan* (compiled by Prince Shao Ming of the Liang Dynasty) which were used as a basis for literary education at the Japanese Imperial University outside Nara. By the mid-eighth century the Japanese state of Yamato was reasonably well-stabilized and of an already high degree of culture. The Japanese people have always, and still do, attach special importance to the art of poetry; and in early Japan, in a manner not unlike the bardic practices of the north Europeans, special classes of persons were trained to memorize what could not be recorded in writing. In 712 one such official of the *Kataribe* (*Reciters Office*), the 65-year-old Hieda no Are, was ordered to re-cite a history of Japan, the *Record of Ancient Matters* (*Kojiki*), to O no

Yasumaro who recorded the recitation in an early form of *manyo-gana*. The task to which Otomo no Yakamochi appears to have been directed by Tachibana no Moroe was a comparable consolidation into written form of the best poetry in Japanese which was then remembered or being spoken throughout Yamato. Obviously, the starting-point for such an undertaking would have been the better of those poems quoted in the *Kojiki* of 712 (and in its later counterpart, the *Nihonshoki* of 720 which, apart from quoted poetry, employed pure Chinese), in the now-lost *Kokashu*, and in the similarly now-lost collections of individual poets. Additionally, Yakamochi drew on the work of his coaeval social equals, notably the poems composed by the literary circle organized by his father Tabito when he was governor-general (725–730) at Dazaifu in Kyushu, the southern city through which all contact with the mainland was channelled. Furthermore, Yakamochi appears to have gone to considerable lengths to collect poetry composed by all sections of Japanese society, so that the *Manyoshu* contains a truly representative range of poetic work: a large number of anonymous poems, many of them love-exchanges (for poems were the normal means of courtship), drinking songs, work songs, poems of Imperial adulation, elegies and funeral songs, exchanges of often comic abuse, poems by professional courtesans and poems of social protest (both by members of the aristocracy expressing their views on social proprieties in accordance with imported Confucian criteria and also by members of the lower classes, especially by the peasantry press-ganged into three-year periods of military service either on the northeastern frontiers around modern Tokyo or to guard the southwestern coastline of Kyushu against possible invasion from the mainland). This considerable volume of lower-class poetry (much of it known to have been collected from conscripts by Yakamochi's agents in 755) is so good that it is almost certain that the original versions were polished up into final form either by Yakamochi

himself or by others of his literary associates. The songs of Shrop-
shire Lads do frequently turn out to have been written by Regius
Professors of classical languages. Nevertheless, the language used in
these conscript poems is undeniably provincial and has given his-
torians of the development of the Japanese language much extremely valuable information; as, for instance, that the language
used in the mid-eighth century employed eight, as opposed to the
current five, vowels. A very few of these conscript poems stand out
in a culture which was fundamentally based on the concept of an
Emperor-ruler (who was both God-descended and himself a God)
by reason of the sheer humanity of their complaints about the heart-
break and disruption of peasant family life occasioned by the
conscriptions.

It follows that a significant proportion of the poetry in the
Manyoshu was composed as part of an oral tradition and carries the
consequent immediate and direct impact, especially in its imagery,
which is associated with oral composition in any poetic tradition.
However, the *Manyoshu* was compiled at a time when poets were
beginning to write their poems down before reciting them or send-
ing them to the appropriate recipients. The later poems in the
anthology, especially those composed in large numbers by Yakamochi himself (who is responsible for a total of 473 poems in the
collection) during his governorship of 746–751 of the province of
Etchu, are of this latter type; and the *Manyoshu* as a whole thus
stands as a marker of the time between the composition of oral
poetry and written poetry. The link between the two types of
poetry is, however, still close and the latter characteristically exploits, even depends upon, the near-magical force (*kotodama*) in the
spoken sound of Yamato words. All poetry ultimately depends
upon the rhythms of incantation, and the poetry of the morning of
the Japanese world lives by that very power.

The anthology now consists of 20 books or scrolls (*maki*), though this vigesimal form of construction was only first mentioned at a much later date by Fujiwara no Michitoshi in his introduction to the *Fourth Imperial Anthology* (the *Goshuishu*) of 1086. The poems mainly derive from the period 259–759, though a few later poems may well have worked their way into the total of 4516 now included in the *Manyoshu*. It contains work by more than 400 named poets, of whom the earliest is the Empress Iwa no Hime who died in 347; but it also includes a large number of anonymous verses which could well have been in verbal circulation from the third, second or even the first century. However, not wishing to overstate the *Manyoshu*'s claim to long antiquity, I have placed such claimants among other anonymous but genuinely later work under a cautious attribution to either the fifth or sixth century. Apart from such early material, the bulk of *Manyoshu* poetry was composed during the period of some 130 years from the reign of the Emperor Jomei (r.629–641) until compilation ceased in 759.

The whole period was one of rapid and often turbulent political development in the islands which we now know as Japan. Those islands' inhabitants were then a mixture of proto-Caucasian Ainu (distinguished by their body hair) and a growing majority of more recent immigrants whose skeletal remains suggest both northeast Asian (Mongolo-Korean) and the southeast Asian (Annamese, south Chinese, possibly even Malayo-Filipino) elements. The Japanese national mythologies strongly indicate a matriarchal Polynesian element among the southerly contribution to the population. By historical times the most recent mixed addition to the population was organized into tribal groups (*uji*) of which the nameless Imperial clan based in the Yamato area had gained through tribal warfare and the support of other main clans and of Korean immigrants an acknowledged supremacy among peer groups. It is, perhaps, worth noting here that in a register of families made in 815, of the 1182 noble families 400 were stated to be of foreign origin. Throughout the four centuries covered by the *Manyoshu* the clans continued to fight among themselves, but the Imperial Yamato state nevertheless, with understandable hiccoughs, maintained its consolidating dominance. The conflict normally took the form of struggles between subordinate clans to advise (and in fact dominate) the Emperor or Empress of the time. These feuds are of ineluctable complexity, but the main theme is the decline of the initially influential military clans under pressure from those clans (especially the sorcerer clan of the *Nakatomi*, who were later honoured with the name of Fujiwara) who master-minded the development of a civil bureaucracy organized in imitation of Chinese practice.

This stretch may conveniently be broken down into four sub-periods: the first from Jomei times around 630 to the Jinshin rebellion of 672; the second from 673 (when the Emperor Temmu came to the throne) until the establishment of the capital at Nara in 710; the third from that establishment until 733 (the so-called period of the Nara Court); and the fourth sub-period from 734 to 759, the so-called Tempyo period of great cultural renown but one in which the stability of aristocratic society was again breaking down.

It is of course impossible to fit the careers of actual poets within the precise limits of these four sub-periods, but these time-slots do roughly correspond to the realities of poetic development. The first sub-period (630–672) was a time of political upheaval directed against the extension of Imperial authority. The folk-song tradition exemplified in the *Kojiki* and *Nihonshoki* was petering out, and poetry was developing into individual lyrical expression in the forms of the *choka* (long song) and *tanka* (short song) which were the first manifestations of a new literary aesthetic. Most of the poets concerned were members of the Imperial family, of whom the best were women poets such as the Empress Saimei (593–661) and especially the Princess Nukada (c.645–c.702) whose brilliant combination of intellect and passion created the first peak in the writing of aristocratic *tanka*.

The second sub-period (673–710) corresponds to a generation of stability reflecting the Emperor Temmu's establishment (with notable military help from the Otomo clan) of bureaucratic government modelled on Chinese practice which would lead to a shift in power from the military clans to those 'fly finaigling aristocrats' best represented by the scheming Fujiwaras. The 'Jinshin energy' generated by the Emperor Temmu and his reforms was expressed in an outburst of romantic feeling and epic poetry which, while maintaining clear links with folk tradition, rejoiced in the benefits of that Imperial dominance which flowed from (and was symbolized in) the completion of the Taiho Code in 710. Again, the typical poets of this sub-period were members of the Imperial family but the greatest poet of them all was Kakinomoto no Hitomaro (c.659– c.712), a man of undistinguished birth who became a low-ranked court official engaged in the production of 'praise-songs' for the Imperial establishment. Almost nothing is known of his life, though it would seem that at some late stage he was given a minor provincial post where, at an undetermined time between 708 and 715, he is believed to have died. His remarkable abilities as a poet have been aptly described as 'a continuous blending of opposite qualities: of the non-individual with the uniquely individual, of the folk-songs of commoners with the self-conscious art of the aristocracy, of the epic with the lyric and of the traditional with the newly-fabricated'.* The *Manyoshu* contains many poems certainly his and it also incorporates the so-called *Hitomaro Collection*, verse closely linked to the folk-song tradition which, if not by Hitomaro himself, is very much in the style he created. He is still regarded by the

* Edward Putzar, *Japanese Literature* (University of Arizona, 1973), adapted from Hisamatsu Sen'ichi's *Nihon Bungaku*.

Japanese as the best of all Manyo poets; and his reputation, if not always the over-laudatory nature of his professional glorifications (hackwork however genuinely felt), justifies his popular designation as a 'saint of poetry' (*Kasei*). I myself find him an excellent poet in his personal poetry but tiresomely sycophantic (though still technically superb) in his official work. The modern critic, Hasegawa Nyozekan, probably goes too far in calling Hitomaro a mere court-functionary whose writing, sadly afflicted with pompous rhetorical flourishes, lacks any real content; but this unpopular line of criticism cannot be dismissed out of hand. Another important poet from this sub-period, whose dates are similarly indeterminable, is Takahashi no Mushimaro who, while showing more obvious Chinese influence than can be seen in Hitomaro, extends the Hitomaro techniques to exploit both legend and popular Japanese song.

The third sub-period, the first 25 years after the establishment of the capital at Nara in 710, was one of further national consolidation which, despite social unrest and suffering among the common people, was one of great sophistication among the court aristocracy and their representatives appointed to provincial governorships. Though folk poetry continued to be composed, poetry as a whole became increasingly urban and self-consciously urbane. The typical poet of the sub-period is Otomo no Tabito, head of that declining military clan, who wrote most of his poetry while serving as Governor General at Dazaifu. Tabito was steeped in Chinese culture, as were his associates (notably his subordinate Governor of Chikuzen, Yamanoue no Okura) in the literary circle which he organized. This group was motivated not so much by ambition to prove that Japanese poetry was the match of anything produced in China (the aim of the later *Manyoshu*) as to demonstrate that provincials could write at least as well as the court poets in the capital at Nara. To achieve that aim they exploited the themes and aesthetics of Chinese poetry, especially that which characterized the Six

Dynasties (222–589), to produce a new kind of Japanese poetry. The group was successful in its members' limited objective, but their work, for all that it exhibited a Chinese influence nowhere else in the *Manyoshu* so clearly shown, became nevertheless a milestone in the development and celebration in poetry of the Japanese spirit. Tabito's elegies (*banka*) on the death of his wife in 728 are subjective expressions of grief which, though certainly reflecting Chinese models, surpass them in lyric intensity and carry a poetic force greater even than that in Hitomaro's elegies either for Imperial personages or for his own loves and family. They are, moreover, the clear source of the superb and undilutedly Japanese lyrics written by his son Yakamochi in lament of the death of his unnamed mistress in 739. Tabito's series of poems in praise of *sake* and drunkenness obviously derive from earlier Chinese poems on that theme but, as expressions of the Japanese attitude to insobriety, they remain unsurpassed to this day. Indeed, their combination of Taoist quietism with Japanese force and good humour remain the best ever celebration of the theme of drunkenness in all world literature. His subordinate Governor and close personal friend, Yamanoue no Okura (660–733), similarly wrote most of his poetry during his provincial spell in Chikuzen in the years 726–732. Okura was equally deep-versed in mainland culture, being a childhood Korean immigrant who had made his way up in Japanese society (including membership of a Japanese embassy to T'ang China in the first decade of the century) by scholarship and industry. Understandably, his nature is less thoroughly Japanese than Tabito's, and his poems in the *Manyoshu* all reflect and evince the depth of his Confucian convictions. In notable contrast to Tabito's devotion to drinking-parties one of Okura's *tanka* shows him breaking away early from such a session in order to get home to his wife and child. Similarly, his longer poems (notably a *choka* built on a dialogue between a poor man and one even more impoverished) show a

Confucian social concern of a depth unrepresented elsewhere in the *Manyoshu*. The third most interesting poet who flowered during this sub-period is the courtier Yamabe no Akahito (who probably died in 736) whom that later doyen of Japanese literary critics, Ki no Tsurayuki (868–946), described in his Preface to the *First Imperial Anthology* of 905 as at least Hitomaro's poetic equal. Akahito is, indeed, essentially a courtier and followed the Hitomaro pattern of praise-poetry for those at the top of the social ladder, but his oeuvre includes remarkable verse on the beauty of nature and the supreme *tanka* celebrating the Japanese aesthetic certainty that the very essence of beauty is its ephemerality.

The fourth sub-period (734–759), though renowned as the culmination of so-called Tempyo culture, was in fact characterized by the collapse into renewed clan-feuding (basically reflecting Fujiwara efforts to attain supreme power) of the overall re-organization of Japan by the Emperor Temmu. In the autumn of 737, when the leaders of all four branches of the Fujiwara clan died in a smallpox epidemic, their main rivals under the leadership of Tachibana no Moroe managed to grasp political control. The Otomo clan, supporters of the Tachibana faction, benefitted by this swing in the power-balance, but the Fujiwara set-back proved brief. Tachibana aspirations were blighted when their candidate to succeed the Emperor Shomu, his son Prince Asaka, died in 745 from blood-poisoning (which was probably of Fujiwara origin) and the Imperial succession passed in 759 to the Emperor's daughter by a Fujiwara woman, the Empress Koken (733–765), who was under the domination of her lover and adviser Fujiwara no Nakamaro. Thereafter Tachibana power vanished: Moroe's son was executed in 759 for participation in a conspiracy against Fujiwara influence, and the Otomo position consequently worsened, as has been noted earlier, to its virtual extinction. It is significant that it was in 759, the year of the Empress Koken's accession, that the last datable poem in the *Manyoshu* was written. The main poet in this fourth and last sub-period of the anthology's coverage is Otomo no Yakamochi himself (718–785). Yakamochi had clearly learnt his poetic craft during his early years in Kyushu when he was in constant contact with the literary circle around his father Tabito. However, he proved expert beyond that circle's expertise in the assimilation of Chinese influences to the creation of new Japanese poetry. His poetic curiosity and inventiveness would have been remarkable at any time, but his natural gifts and his applied intelligence made him the obvious choice when Tachibana no Moroe was looking around for a man capable of organizing a body of Japanese poetry of a quality matching the Chinese verse with which the Court was already familiar. Much of the poetry ultimately incorporated in the *Manyoshu*, some tenth of it being of Yakamochi's own composition, would already have been in the possession of the Otomo clan; and Yakamochi was well placed to collect more material, both of traditional and of court origin, for inclusion in the eventually vast collection. A particular circumstance strengthening his position in this matter was that his father's half-sister, the Lady Otomo no Sakanoue (699–c.781), was the best woman poet so far then to have emerged in Japan. Since his teens Yakamochi had exchanged poems with this gifted aunt who, from about 747, was also his mother-in-law and who, from Tabito's death in 731 until Yakamochi himself took over in 754, was the head of the whole Otomo clan. Her poetry exhibits not only the sophistication and wit of a Tempyo court lady but also the general organizational skills of a major clan leader living in particularly tricky times. Though Yakamochi managed to survive the crisis of 759 and even thereafter received a variety of government appointments, including two minor provincial governorships (an occupation in which so much Manyo poetry had been written), those appointments were all of less importance than those he had held when young and he appears to have written no more poems in the 26 years before his death in 785.

Mention of the Lady Sakanoue provides a convenient opportunity to comment upon the representation of women poets in the *Manyoshu*, a representation indicated by asterisks against their listing among the authors of poems in the contents pages of the present book. The position of women in Manyo and earlier times is difficult to determine by reason of the lack of detailed records, and what information we do possess tends understandably to concentrate upon the circumstances of the land- and other property-owning classes in which, significantly, women could both own and inherit property. But even women lower in the social scale were not yet burdened by wide Japanese acceptance either of the Chinese Confucian code (under which any woman's life was controlled successively by her father, her husband and her eldest son) or of Buddhist beliefs (under which women were inherently inferior to men, and could indeed only hope by outstanding merit to progress to reincarnation in male form). It seems likely that a significant element of the islands' population had originated in Polynesia and brought with them matriarchal, even matrilineal, cultural patterns. There were eight periods of Empress-rule between 593 and 769, and the Empress Saimei died in 661 at the point of leading armies against the mainland Chinese. Certainly the women poets of the Manyo period were no wilting lilies. Their many poems in the anthology show them to have been strikingly independent-minded and, as already mentioned, the Lady Sakanoue successfully headed the Otomo military clan for 23 difficult years. Together with the Princess Nukada (c.645–c.700), she stands at the head of a long line of first-rate women poets which stretches on through Ono no Komachi, Izumi Shikibu and the Princess Shikishi to Yosano Akiko and today's Shiraishi Kazuko.

★ ★ ★

Though the translations in this book must stand or fall on their own feet, some comment on the poetic forms of the original Japanese material in the *Manyoshu* may be of interest. The earliest, and many later, critics of the anthology categorized its contents not by poetic form but, apparently in imitation of Chinese practice, into three groups: miscellaneous poems (*zoka*), love poetry (*somonka*) and elegies (*banka*). This is a sensible approach, but categorization by poetic form is nevertheless a viable alternative. The translations in this present book have been selected for their quality, both as poems-in-Japanese and as poems-in-English; and, disregarding their ordering in the standard edition of the *Manyoshu* itself, have been arranged (so far as possible) in chronological order of their authors' birth-dates. The earliest poems in the collection are, in fact, formless; and that very absence of any established Japanese form was cited as a precedent by twentieth-century Japanese poets when they began imitating the formlessness of modern Western poetry. However, Japanese poetic practice (natural expressions of the nature of the Japanese language) soon centred upon syllabic count in various patterns of five and seven syllables. Experiments with rhyme, both in comparatively early times and indeed by Otomo no Yaka-mochi himself in imitation of Chinese practice and again in the twentieth century in imitation of Western poetry, all failed because virtually every Japanese word ends in one of its few vowels so that rhyme is so easy as to be ineffective as a poetic device. In Manyo times the use of the five and seven syllabic rhythm evolved into several regular patterns, of which it is simplest first to consider the long poem (*choka*) which contains any number of 5:7 syllable couplets with a final couplet of 7:7 syllables. The *choka* probably began in imitation of the similar long Chinese rhapsody (*fu*) or the Korean long poem (*hyang-ga*); and, just as both those forms customarily ended with a summarizing envoy (*luan* and *hugu* respectively), so the *choka* developed a summarizing *hanka*. The *hanka* in its independent form as short poem (*tanka*) became the commonest Manyo form, and indeed the commonest form in the whole history of Japanese prosody and its total of 31 syllables, written in one or two vertical lines, are built into a pattern of five units in 5 : 7 : 5 : 7 : 7 syllables. The *Manyoshu* contains some 260 *choka* and nearly 4200 *tanka*. The collection also contains 62 'head-repeated poems' (*sedoka*) organized in six units of 5 : 7 : 7 : 5 : 7 : 7 syllables, and a single 'Buddha's footprint poem' (*bussokuseki katai*) organized, like a *tanka* with one additional seven-syllable unit, in the pattern of 5 : 7 : 5 : 7 : 7 : 7 syllables. To complete the picture, one should add that the work also contains a single *renga* (linked poem) in *tanka* form and some work in Chinese and in Chinese poetic form.

I should also add that the translations make no attempt to echo the original Japanese poetic forms which, though natural outgrowths of the Japanese language, are not natural outgrowths of English. The relation between the forms of the originals and of their translations is that both are traditional and that both are natural expressions of the languages concerned. Though I possess a certain expertise, both as a university scholar and as a linguist, I make no claims in those respects when it comes to making translations of poetry; for it seems to me that the one essential qualification for translating poetry is to be oneself a poet.

Inasmuch as poetry is the quintessence of a particular language, it is by definition untranslatable – even between related languages. Consequently the 'translator' should aim to create in his mother tongue (the receptor-language) a poem having the same effect as the original had upon natural users of the donor-language. The original poem will be written in poetic forms that are essentially expressions of the nature of the donor-language, but that are rarely natural expressions of the nature of the receptor-language. Thus, to try to translate a *tanka* (a five-unit form comprising 31 syllables organized in a rhythmic pattern natural to the Japanese language) into a five-unit English poem is to try to force a highly emotional Japanese poem into a form that in English, has the comic (and certainly unsophisticated) effect of the five-line limerick. At least the limerick exploits the rhyme patterns natural in English, whereas most academics who publish translations of *tanka* do so in five un-rhymed lines that, even when fangled into a total of 31 English syllables, lack any sense of poetic craftsmanship in English. The five-line pattern adopted by most such 'literalist' translators of *tanka* into English is, in technical fact, an error: for the originals, though composed in five-syllabic units, are normally written in one (sometimes two) lines. The five-line structure was only popularized in Japanese practice as recently as 1910 in Ishikawa Takuboku's *Handful of Sand*.

After prolonged experiments with various English poetic forms, I came to the conclusion that a traditionally structured Japanese poem can best be rendered into an equivalently traditional English poetic form; and that the poetic effects of Japanese syllabic rhythm (memorability, tight coherence and, at the end, a clinching finality) are best achieved by the use of rhyme in English.

For the translation of *tanka* the most suitable English form would seem to be the loose sextain. Use of the quatrain produces an epigrammatic effect not natural to the original, but there are occasions when the quatrain, even the quintain, does achieve an effect equivalent to that of the original *tanka*; however, in my experience the shorter English forms only become appropriate when the original is itself sloppy in its Japanese construction.

I began making translations at the request of the *Asahi Shimbun*'s English-language quarterly review (the *Japan Quarterly*) that, at the time concerned (c.1965), wanted English-language versions of modern Japnese poetry. It soon became clear that modern Japanese poetry, even more than classical Japanese poetry, evoked multi-level reactions (both in respect of semantic content and in respect of

emotional impact) among its Japanese readers. In an effort to grasp
the full poetic effect of such poetry, I began assembling comments
on any selected poem from (on average) ten Japanese people, five of
each sex, ranging in social and intellectual status from coolies to
mandarins, from bar girls to university professors, from airline
crews to practising poets.

These comments produced a fairly general consensus with respect to semantic content of the selected poem but a much wider
range of emotional and associative reaction in respect of the feelings
aroused by the original Japanese text. Since a good poem makes its
effect across the whole spectrum of speakers of the language concerned, I concluded that any good English translation must make
an equivalent impact across a similar range of English-language
speakers; so that, once I had grasped the effect of the Japanese original on a wide range of Japanese readers, I scrapped all my pre-
liminary work and endeavoured to write a poem-in-English that
would have the equivalent effect on a similar range of English
readers. At the risk of making a mere phrase, I was in fact seeking to
translate, from Japanese into English, not so much the poem as the
poetry.

The results inevitably led the more literal-minded and academic
critics to complain that my English versions often differed widely
from the literal Japanese original texts. However, I remain certain
that my approach was sound (though I myself might well be an
indifferent poet in English), especially after Ito Sei (a personal friend
of and something of an authority on the great modern Japanese
poet Hagiwara Sakutaro) told me at a meeting of the Japan PEN
Club in Tokyo that, having checked my versions against Hagiwara
originals, those portions of my version that he had marked as 'real
Hagiwara' proved not to be literal translations while those portions
that were indeed accurate literal translations he had marked as
'cardboard Hagiwara'. At all events, thus given heart by the ap-

proval of Japanese poets, I felt and still feel disinclined to pay much heed to the carping of academics, but rather take comfort from the waspish Sei Shonagon who knew what she was doing when in one of her devastating 'lists' she lumped together walnuts, knotweed, prickly water lilies, and Doctors of Literature.

The technique of making translations described in the preceding paragraphs, though it had been developed in respect of modern poems, proved applicable to all periods of Japanese poetry; indeed, I have also used it in respect of verse from other languages. I simply do not believe that literal translations can ever translate poetry; for, if they could, any competent linguist with a lexicon could present himself as a master poet in the receptor-language. Versions of Ono no Komachi in scholar-perfect English can be linguistically exact; but, considered as poetry, they are peach stones presented as evidence of the exquisite flavour of peach flesh. Jonathan Swift, in his *Letter to a Young Poet*, commented that 'Shakespeare had been a worse poet had he been a better Scholar' and referred to the poet's happy lack of even so much 'real learning as would cover a sixpence in the bottom of a Bason'. Linguists are not poets, and scholars are not poets; and, in my view, poetry usually suffers from their attentions. One cannot read the heart with the head. And if one has not 'heart' in the Japanese sense of that word, then Japanese poetry is incommunicable.

Inevitably, even the most spectacularly successful translation of the poetry in the *Manyoshu* cannot recreate in English the life, the freshness, the quivering energy of the originals; for the anthology's poetry from the morning of the Japanese world is so intensely alive as in fact to be timeless, and the world of which it tells remains forever the world of the present indicative. Its combination of impassioned lyrical singing and a certain rumbustious directness reflect both the vitality and the earthiness of the Japanese people before their native vigour and sincerity (*makoto*) were modified, and perhaps distorted, by successive overlays of Chinese sophistication.

★ ★ ★

It is customary in concluding such introductions, while accepting one's own total responsibility for whatever the book contains, to offer thanks to those persons and institutions without whose assistance the work could never have been completed. In the present case I owe so much to so many that it would be invidious to mention even the most helpful. However, I feel I must express my gratitude to the Tokyo Metropolitan Police and to their colleagues at the base of the Noto Peninsula for the extraordinary lengths to which they went to help me in identifying the old and modern place names along the route flown on or just before 3 November 747 by Otomo no Yakamochi's errant hawk Okuro (Sir Black). I think it reflects a national devotion to and recognition of the importance of poetry that, in response to my request for information, a police car and two officers were despatched to follow, making enquiries along the travelled way, that lost bird's route. I doubt whether any similar request for help from the police in Britain or the States would meet with a like understanding or response.

Graeme Wilson
Exmouth, June 1991

FROM THE MORNING OF THE WORLD

BEREAVEMENT

Shimmering above the golden
Paddies thick with ripened grain,
The mists of morning thin to nothing.

But how shall this, the marrow-pain
Of my loneliness without him,
Ever be dispersed again?

Empress Iwa no Hime (−347)

ASSIGNATION

Here, at the ford which budding willows
Overhang and half-surround,
I, that should be drawing water,
Hang around and hang around.

Look, my heel-prints of impatience
Half-mooned on the patient ground.

Anonymous (fifth or sixth century)

BLOWN

After an age of courtship
I stand before her door,
At long long last accepted
But too wearied to go more
Like a horse blown by a nine-mile gallop
On the pebbles of a shingle-shore.

Anonymous (fifth or sixth century)

GOSSIP

Like the sound of oars at Konga ferry,
Their sliding slap, their smack and shove,
Ill-founded gossip laps around us:
We who never yet made love.

Anonymous (fifth or sixth century)

HANDS

These hands so chapped with pounding rice:
Tonight again he'll groan,
The young lord of the manor
As he takes them in his own.

Anonymous (fifth or sixth century)

NEIGHBOURLINESS

You keep on saying she's a wife.
So what?
You've borrowed clothes from neighbours,
Have you not?

Anonymous (fifth or sixth century)

ON THE MARCH

So far we've marched, so many miles
My need for her is numb.

Comrade, do not melt the stony
Coldness I've become
With talk of wife and children,
The lost warm world of home.

Anonymous (fifth or sixth century)

PILLOW TALK

'Oh yes,' she says, 'we're married:
Very much so,' says she
Wedging the bed-clothes under her hip,
Turning her back on me.

Anonymous (fifth or sixth century)

RAINBOW

Let everybody know we love.
Who cares if it should show
Plain as the rainbow spanning the weir
Across the Ikaho?
If only I may sleep with you,
Who cares how many know?

Anonymous (fifth or sixth century)

REMEMBRANCE

On winter evenings when the mist hangs low
Over the reed-beds and the reeds look blue
And chill, chill, chill
                    the wild ducks call each other,
I shall remember you.

Anonymous (fifth or sixth century)

SLANDER

Like driftwood in the roaring rapids,
Helpless in its vicious flow,
Down the cataract of slander,
Willy-nilly, here we go.

Anonymous (fifth or sixth century)

OLD WOMAN

How could a woman old as I,
An old old woman, come to be
So dunced by love that puling tots
Seem wise old men compared with me.

Lady Ishikawa (early seventh century)

INVITATION

Lover, come. Squeeze gently through
These hanging blinds of split bamboo.
If my mother calls *What's that?* –
Mother of the breasts gone flat –
Mother, I shall make reply,
The night-wind, Mother, blowing by.

Anonymous (early seventh century)

Is that you, for whom I've waited,
You for whom I've pined
With all the fevers of the flesh,
The hungers of the mind?

Only the mindless wind of autumn
Fretting the bamboo blind.

Princess Nukada (c.645–c.702)

DAWN

The eastern fields, soft-glowing, wear
The first pink flush of day.
I look behind me. Lonely there
The white moon sinks away.

Kakinomoto no Hitomaro (c.659–712)

When I leave my love behind me
In the hills of Hikité,
When from her small and stony grave
Stonily I walk away,
When along the little pathway
Running down the mountainside
I walk down, it is as though
I that walk had also died.

Kakinomoto no Hitomaro (c.659–712)

MOUNTAIN WIZARD

This figure of a mountain wizard
Carries both furs and fan
As if to show that timelessness
Began when time began.

Summer is winter, winter summer.
Ah, what a knowing man.

Kakinomoto no Hitomaro (c.659–712)

THE CHILDREN

Whenever I eat melon
How the children leap to mind!
And, again, when I eat chestnuts
Every mouthful wakes the grind
Of my loneliness without them.

They invade my sleep. They make
Such a business of my dreaming
I spend half the night awake.

So what care I for silver,
Precious metals, precious stone?
What greater wealth than children
Can a man expect to own?

Yamanoue no Okura (660–733)

Those plum-slips that we planted,
My darling wife and I,
Stand now in the garden
As thick around and high
As full-grown trees.

                    I stare at them.

How high their branches float
Upon these tears which blind me
As grief thickens in my throat.

Otomo no Tabito (665–731)

If, here and now, I'm happy,
It were indeed absurd
To worry lest, in some next life,
I prove an ant or bird.

Otomo no Tabito (665–731)

BIRTH WISH

Well, if I must be born again,
Let my being be
Re-bodied as a saké-jar
That that next tenancy
Of form may be a form where wine
Can soak itself in me.

Otomo no Tabito (665–731)

THE BEACH AT SUMINOÉ

Do not cut these reed-beds.
From where else could I watch
The girls go by in scarlet skirts
Wave-wet to the crotch?

Anonymous (late seventh century)

DISAVOWAL

Because I had no answer
For the other people here,
People who were bound to ask
'And who was that, my dear?',
Through tears I told your messenger
He'd got the wrong address.

I trust that those reported tears
Conveyed my answer yes.

Anonymous (late seventh century)

No. I shall not die for love.
I lack the discipline
To face the waves and drown in them.
My nature is to spin
Around and around like a grain of sand
Whenever a tide flows in.

Anonymous (late seventh century)

We parted: but, half-hoping
She might perhaps relent,
She might perhaps have spoken words
She had not really meant,
Over my shoulder, now and then,
I looked back as I went.

Anonymous (late seventh century)

LONELINESS

Darling, when you do not come
My world becomes a blur
Of loneliness so bitter
It would sharpen vinegar.

Yet, if you do come, afterwards
One feels yet lonelier.

Anonymous (late seventh century)

MODESTY

You claim to be so modest
And I will not say you lie,
But no one wears a scarlet skirt
Expecting to get by
Without attracting notice
From the quicker kinds of eye.

Anonymous (late seventh century)

NEED

There is, I think, no single hour
In which I do not find
Myself brief-swept with need for you.

But in the evenings, blind
With love and longing, there's no other
Matter in my mind.

Anonymous (late seventh century)

ONE THAT GOT AWAY

So self-assured, so certain that
No girl I loved could leave me flat,
Back to back, as stiff as two
Person-lengths of split bamboo,
Fool that I was, I dared agree
To sleep that night she slept with me.

Anonymous (late seventh century)

PLEASANTRIES

The pleasant things you said were said
As much, no doubt, to ease
The savageries of silence
As they were said to please:
But when one learns the truth, what use
Are all such pleasantries?

Anonymous (late seventh century)

SUN-BEAR RAPIDS

If, as we cross the rapids,
I reach an arm to guide
This girl who could not elsewise come
Safe to the other side,
Must gossip tongues discredit kindness
Into something snide?

Anonymous (late seventh century)

SURPRISE

Heart-warming, when I visit
Unannounced, is her surprise.

Promises are merely words
And words are often lies,
But O her lifted eyebrows
and the shining in her eyes.

Anonymous (late seventh century)

TROTH

Standing under the orange-tree
She reached for a lower spray,
Broke it off and offered it
For me to take away.

What more, though not a word was said,
Had we the need to say?

Anonymous (late seventh century)

TRYST

I told them I was waiting
To see the white moon rise
Over the mountain's shoulder.

What a pack of lies
I told them as I waited
For the true light of my eyes.

Anonymous (late seventh century)

Under the broad vermilion bridge
Clear shining waters flow:
Over its stretch, uncompanied,
A girl walks to and fro,
Her trailing skirt bright crimson,
Her cloak dark indigo.

Has she a husband, supple, young
As spring's fresh greennesses?
Or is her sleep so acorn-single
None may call her his?

I long to ask, but know not even
Where her dwelling is.

Had I here beside this bridge
A dwelling of my own,
I would offer shelter, greet her,
Let my name be known
To one so lost, so wistful-looking
Walking there alone.

Takahashi no Mushimaro (late seventh century)

With what should I compare this world?
With the white wake left behind
A ship that dawn watched row away
Out of its own conceiving mind.

Priest Manzei (c.670–c.730)

IF IT WERE DEATH

If it were death to love,
Dear love, believe you me
A thousand times a thousand times
I shall have lived to see
My mortal flesh bear witness
To its immortality.

Lady Kasa (–733)

SWORD

I dreamt, and in my dream
Quite clearly I could see,
Laid at my side, a long straight sword.

What could its meaning be?

Could such a dream perhaps foretell
You'll be visiting me?

Lady Kasa (–733)

CHERRY BLOSSOMS

The essence of their beauty
Is that it dies away
So exquisitely quickly.

How could one possibly pay
Even respect to a flower in flower
Day upon day upon day?

Yamabe no Akahito (–736)

Since by the time the moon's white pearl
Was full grown in the sky
You'd still not come, what could I do
But turn to sleep and try
There to give you all that love
You could not there deny?

Lady Otomo no Sakanoue (699–c. 781)

In the shadow of a thicket
On this summer-wasted land,
Their startling flowers unremarked,
The red-star lilies stand.

To burn with love, and yet to be
Not even noticed. Agony.

Lady Otomo no Sakanoue (699–c.781)

Abrim with its sense of the world's wild wonder
Manifest in you,
I feel my heart like a running river
Which, and whatever I do
To dam and double-dam its flow,
Nevertheless breaks through.

Lady Otomo no Sakanoue (699–c.781)

UNDERSTANDINGS

You said 'I'll come,' but did not:
So now, because you said
'I will not come,' I think you will.

Or have I still mis-read
The alternations of your heart,
Your flibbertigibbety head?

Lady Otomo no Sakanoue (699–c.781)

I deal with them politely:
At least I hope I do.

At least I dealt politely
With the first fool one or two,
But send me no more messengers
When I have asked for you.

Otomo no Yotsuna (early eighth century)

NO

It's not because I'm now too old,
More wizened than you guess . . .

If I say no, it's only
Because I fear that yes
Would bring me nothing, in the end,
But a fiercer loneliness.

Lady Ki no Washika (early eighth century)

No one dives to the ocean-bottom
Just like that:
One does not learn the skills involved
At the drop of a hat.

It's those skills slow-learnt in the depths of love
That I'm working at.

Lady Nakatomi (early eighth century)

RED SKIRT

Outside, that gentle drizzle
Will be moulding to her skin
My wife's red skirt.
                    It would be downright
Crazy to stay in.

Anonymous (early eighth century)

SUMMER GRASS

My love-thoughts are like summer grass
In these long days of rain:
No sooner scythed and raked away
But up they come again,
Fiercely alive with all the coarse
Green energies of pain.

Anonymous (early eighth century)

Old legend has it that a doe which mates
With lespedeza drops but a single fawn.

Today my fawn-sole son, my only child,
Sets forth on that long road where every dawn
Will find him pillowed upon grass.
                              That he may travel
Safe through all peril on his journeyings,
First cleansed with ritual water, I have threaded
This hanging thrave of clean-cut bamboo-rings
And then set out, correctly swathed in cloths
Woven from mulberry-bark, these jars of wine,
These sacred jars, therewith to supplicate
Divine protection for that fawn of mine.

When night-frost crackles on those open fields
Where, bivouaced against the cold it brings,
Our mission huddles, warm around my darling,
O white birds flocked from heaven, fold your wings.

Mother of a Mission-member (written in 733)

Some other time, you tell me:
Not now; perhaps; we'll see.

Knowing you've no intention
Of anything with me,
I think I'd think you kinder
For a no's flat honesty.

Ki no Toyokawa (written in 739)

WHO?

There was, they said,
Some person just come back:
I could not catch just who.
But, as I listened,
Love, my heart turned over
Hoping it might be you.

Sanu Chigami (written in 740)

Here is a man loose-clothed in plain white cloth
Homespun, no doubt, from hemp his own wife grew.

This man, so shrunk his sash goes round him thrice,
Set out, his service done, hard service too,
To see his parents, to rejoin his wife
And so, ill-coated, shivering, he came
To climb this savage pass; to Ashigara.

Ask as you may, he will not tell his name,
He will not tell you who his kinfolk are
Nor yet the place where he was born and bred.

Black hair blown loose, white hemp-cloth wind-aflicker,
Here on his journey he lies cold and dead.

Tanabe no Fukumaro (fl.c.748)

HAND

I lift my hand. I stare at it.
This is the hand you pressed
So pledgefully that time we lay,
Ours only, breast to breast,
And pledged each other love eternal.

Staring at my hand,
I drown in understandings
That I dare not understand.

Lady Heguri (written c.750)

Seven big-wheeled wagons
Were not enough to cart
These shining sheaves of love-thoughts,
This harvest of my heart:
Seven wagons big enough
Never could be found
To take the weight of happiness
My heart can carry round.

Princess Hirokawa (written c.750)

COMFORT

'Good luck, lad,' they told me:
'Come home safe,' they said.

I shall never forget my parents' words
As they placed their hands on my head
And gave me comfort; they who needed
Most to be comforted.

Hasetsukabe no Inamaro (written in 755)

CONSCRIPT

As from today, I tell myself,
As from to-bloody-day
They're shipping me off to the ends of the world
To be a shield, they say,
Guarding the goddam Emperor
From a thousand miles away.

Imamatsuribe no Yosafu (written in 755)

AGEING

O that the stairs to heaven
Stretched further than they stretch:
Were but the tallest mountain
Yet taller, I would fetch
Those far-off waters from the moon
Whose magic would restore
The ardours of his youth and make
My man a man once more.

It breaks the heart to watch
One who is more to me
Than all the lights in heaven sink
Towards senility.

Anonymous (eighth century)

A man lies dead on a beach
Which only birds frequent.
In the background, mountains;
At his feet, the spent
Spume of the sea; and seaweeds
Curled to his careless head.

Ask his name and dwelling,
Nothing will be said:
But somewhere wife and children,
Waiting for him, say
Soon now he'll be back with us,
Today, for sure today.

Anonymous (eighth century)

FISHING LANTERNS

As down behind the mountain-rim
The moon begins to sink,
Across these wide dark wastes of water
Fishing lanterns blink
And, when we think ourselves alone
Far out on the midnight sea,
There comes the sound of plashing oars
Yet farther out than we.

Anonymous (eighth century)

Within that filthy hovel
Which I would gladly burn,
On fouled and ragged matting
A rubbish heap might spurn,
There on her grimed and greasy arm,
Arm that I'd joy to break,
There on her arm my darling sleeps
While I lie wide awake;
While all day long and all night long,
Dark nights as long as weeks,
I groan and cry and thresh about
Until the flooring creaks.

Burning! It is I who burn,
I whose burning heart
Impels these empty arms and hands
To rip the world apart.

Anonymous (eighth century)

With that trust which one puts in a great ship
My trust was stark and stern
That some day this benighted month
My true love would return
Till a messenger brought rumour, rumour
Vague as a glow-worm's glow,
That my true love was lost, was gone
As the leaves of autumn go.

This cold earth that I tread upon
Is now an earth of flame;
Whether I sit or whether I stand
The burning is the same.
Lost in blind bewilderment,
My sighs are eight feet long
And, aimless as the morning mist,
All my roads prove wrong.

Ah, if I could find the place
Where my true love lies,
Gladly would I, like a cloud,
Wander in the skies;
Gladly, like the stricken deer,
Die if death would show
How to find him, where to join him,
Which the road to go.

Alas, there seems no answer.
Grief-broken and grief-bowed,
I loiter here in lone bereavement
Crying my grief aloud
For, watching the wings of the skimming wild-geese
Over the reed-beds splayed,
I remember that shape behind his back
Which his quivered arrows made.

Anonymous (eighth century)

ORANGE TREE

It's fair, I would agree,
That you should reckon me
Unworthy of regard:
But will you not come see
The flowering orange-tree
Blanching my whole back-yard?

Anonymous (eighth century)

Some village woman told me
Her husband had seen mine
Riding, haggard, on a jet-black horse
Under the scarlet shine
Of autumn leaves on Kamunabi.

She said he saw him ride
Through falling leaves to vanish where
The seven streams divide.

I had not asked that woman
For news of any sort:
Why should she set my heart on edge
With such a strange report?

Anonymous (eighth century)

SHAME

My lord, you have brought upon me
Shame which I cannot face.

I am going back to the Asuka River
Which, in my native place,
Runs cold enough and deep enough
To cleanse me of disgrace.

Princess Yashiro (written in 758)

Tamana lived at Sué:
What a lass was she
With her breast broad and her waist as narrow
As that of a belted bee.

She'd no need to beckon.
When she simply stood
Smiling flower-like by her door
Total strangers would,
As though entranced, be drawn to her;
And one fool neighbour-man,
Turning his own wife out of doors,
Uninvited ran
To give Tamana all his keys.

No man could resist
So warm, so undemanding
A sunny sensualist.

For, to Tamana, need was all:
Not manliness, not pay.
And no man who approached her door
At any time of day,
At any time of day or night,
Was ever turned away.

Anonymous (eighth century)

I wait and wait. He does not come.
The wild geese coldly cry.
The night grows late and yet more late
And, from a freezing sky,
The wind blows hard. It turns to ice
This snow upon my sleeves,
And ground-frost hardens to a crust
Of frozen grass and leaves.

On such a night he'll never come.
How could he come? Instead,
Hoping at least I'll dream he came,
I shiver back to bed.

Anonymous (eighth century)

Is he here? Is he back? I asked them:
No one seemed to know.

I ran outside to look for him
As fast as I could go,
Into an empty courtyard
And the sibilance of snow.

Anonymous (eighth century)

WOMAN

That girl I took into an empty house
And loved a fortnight there
Is now grown up. Like other women,
Demure and debonair,
She glories in the glossiness
Of once-dishevelled hair.

Anonymous (eighth century)

WORLD ENOUGH

I have lived too long in this hovel of a world,
In temporal distress,
To waste more time in longing for Nirvana's
Infinite nothingness.

Anonymous (eighth century)

DEAR LADY

You seem, dear lady, to have been
Living in Eternity.

Where but in that Timeless Land
Could you thus have grown to be
More young than when, long years ago,
Last you deigned to dazzle me?

Otomo no Miyori (−774)

BAMBOO FENCE

The fence, I said, may need repair:
New bindings, fresh bamboo.
I'll just go down and check, I said,
What one may need to do.

That's what I said. I went, of course,
In hope of seeing you.

Otomo no Yakamochi (718–785)

FRINGED PINKS

That I might not forget her
This lonely autumntide,
The fringed pinks which she planted
In the beds on either side
Of the stone-paved walk are all in bloom
As though she had not died.

Otomo no Yakamochi (718–785)

Moroto tells me, over and over,
Over and over again,
How much she loves me.
                         Ah, Moroto,
How many have lain
Here in your arms, as drunk as I
Upon lie-champagne.

Otomo no Yakamochi (718–785)

Come autumn with its frost and dews
When wild birds gather into flocks
Among the combes and coppices,
The brushwood-thickets, thorn and box,
Then, riding with my honoured friends,
I'd bring Sir Black, my bellicose
Black giant of an arrow-tail
Whom, from an hundred hawks, I chose
To wear my silver-coated bells.

Perfect in form, his appetite
For pure ferocity was such
He'd scare five hundred birds to flight
In one brief morning, double that
On the same evening. Never once
Did quarry marked by my Sir Black
Survive his plummet-stooping pounce.
All that he did was nonpareil:
Coming, going, on my glove,
His matchlessness evoked in me
A pride less pride than aching love.

One day my fat-head falconer
Without so much as an if-I-may
Unperched Sir Black and went off hawking
On, of all daft days, a day
Of falling rain and low dark cloud.

Coughing when he reported back,
'He flew,' that fool Yamada said,
'Across the moors towards the wrack
Of clouds above the mountain-crest
And there, still climbing, sailed from sight.'

What could I do? I was not even
Certain of his line of flight
Since to believe that fool Yamada
Half the time one won't be right
And no man finds an errant hawk
In thickening rain and failing light.

My heart within me felt as though
It were some grate where anger burned:
I sighed whole gales, I fumed, I wept,
I even prayed he be returned.
On both sides of that baleful mountain
Guards were posted, nets were spread
And, that the gods might grant me luck,
Cloths woven from the finest thread
And, gladly, my great polished mirror
Were sent as offerings to the shrine.

Again I prayed, I prayed and waited:
Ah, that great black hawk of mine.

And then it happened in my dreams
That a girl appeared and made this speech:
'That splendid bird you so much miss,
As it flew west along the beach
Of Pinefield Bay, was overtaken
By the still faster wings of night.
Next day he crossed by Ice View Creek,
Those sprat-bright waters, to alight
On Good Luck Island. Two days back
And then again but yesterday
I watched him cruise above the mallards
Flocked in that inlet of the Bay
Where, two years back, he first was captured.
Do not despair. That hawk you seek
In two days at the earliest
And, at the worst, within a week
Will fly fierce-hearted home once more.'

So, in my dream, that young girl spoke
The words I needed to hear spoken
And thus was happy when I woke.

But weeks and weeks have now gone by
With that black apple of my eye
Still vagrant in the wintering sky.

An hundred and ten times over
I'd sell Yamada's skin
To have that hawk back on my wrist
As the winter closes in.

Otomo no Yakamochi (718–785)

Spring. The garden. Peach-trees
Fabulously red.
A path between them where a girl,
As through a flower-bed,
Wades in the lane's reflection
Of the flowers overhead.

Otomo no Yakamochi (718–785)

Empress Iwa no Hime (c.296–347)
Empress-Consort of the sixteenth Emperor Nintoku (290–399).
Both the early Japanese histories (the *Kojiki* of 712 and the *Nihon Shoki* of 720) contain stories woven around the poems exchanged between Emperor and Empress; but no truly reliable historical information survives. Writing was not officially in use until 405, and the compilation of the earliest records did not begin until 682.

Lady Ishikawa (seventh century)
There are several women poets of this name whose work is included in the *Manyoshu*. However, the poem 'Old Woman' appears to have been written by a lady-in-waiting in the palace of Prince Otsu (663–686) who was a son of the fortieth Emperor Temmu (622–686). The poem probably came into the possession of the Otomo clan because it was addressed to a clan-member of that period.

Princess Nukada (c.645–702)
She was the daughter of Prince Kagami. She was a favourite successively of Prince Oama (the future fortieth Emperor Temmu) and, around 660, of his older brother (the future thirty-eighth Emperor Tenchi, 626–671). Her complicated relationship with two brothers called for great social skills, and she was no less skilful in the composition of poetry: she is indeed accepted as the first in a long line of major Japanese poetesses.

Kakinomato no Hitomaro (c.659–c.712)
Nothing is known of this poet (even the suggested life-dates are largely conjectural), except that from the head-notes to, and the contents of, his surviving poems. He appears to have been of undis-

tinguished birth and to have served as a lowly official in the train of successive rulers, both the forty-first Empress Jito (646–703) and the forty-second Emperor Mommu (683–707), as a Court praise-singer. Though his consequently incessant adulation of members of the Imperial family falls a little flat on most modern ears, he was an undoubtedly skilful poet and is still generally held to deserve the poetic supremacy implied in his designation as *Kasei*, a 'saint of poetry'. He contrived to combine traditional praise-poetry with brilliant original imagery, and his 'unofficial' poetry is remarkable for its lyric intensity. He is believed to have had two wives, of whom one was herself an excellent poetess.

Yamanoue no Okura (660–733)
This poet was almost certainly of Korean origin, and is thought to have come to Japan as a boy when his father fled the oppression of Buddhists in Paekche. Immigration of cultured Koreans was welcomed by the authorities of the developing Yamato State in Japan. Okura appears slowly to have made his way upwards in Japanese society by assiduous study and scholarship: thus in 702 he was the most junior member (secretary to Ambassador Awada no Mahito) of a Japanese embassy to the Tang Court at Changan. The 160-man mission left for home in 704 in separate parties, of whom only a third reached Japan, some taking as long as sixteen years to arrive. In 714 Okura was advanced fourteen court ranks from the lowest grading which, together with the Japanese name Yamanoue, he had been granted in 702; and in 716 was even made a minor provincial governor (of Hoki). In 721 he became a tutor to the Crown Prince (later the forty-fifth Emperor Shomu) and, in the period 726–732, governor of the important province of Chikuzen. In this last post he was in close and friendly touch with the leading poet Otomo no Tabito (665–731) who was then Governor-general of the southernmost island of Kyushu. In 732 Okura returned to Nara

where, next year, he died. The *Manyoshu* contains 51 *tanka*, ten *choka* and one *sedoka* by Okura; and he is probably the author of a series of poems on the 'Fisher Folk of Shiga', a part of Chikuzen. The *Manyoshu* further records two poems by Okura in Chinese, and mentions that he compiled the now lost *Ruiju Karin* (*Forest of Classified Verse*). He is singular among Manyo poets for his Paekche-style Buddhism and the pervasiveness of Chinese attitudes of mind, which are most clearly seen in his criticism of social matters, especially of poverty among the lower classes.

Otomo no Tabito (665–731)
He was the eldest son of his Major Counseller (*dainagon*) father and, in due course, succeeded Yasumaro as head of the Otomo clan. This basically military clan, though still influential, was already in decline, its military dominance passing to the Mononobe clan (and eventually to the Minamotos, 'the teeth and claws of the Fujiwaras'); while its civil power was on the wane as the Fujiwara clan continued its rise to ultimate centuries-long total control of the nation. Comparatively late in life, in 720, Tabito was made a General and successfully put down a revolt by the Hayato peoples (whom the Imperial authorities regarded as 'barbarians') in Southern Kyushu. In recognition of his military success, he was appointed in 725/6 head of the *Dazaifu*, the government centre of Kyushu which controlled both the elaborate defences against invasion from the mainland and the passage to the capital at Nara of all foreign visitors. In 730 he achieved his father's rank of *dainagon* and became one of four second-rank Imperial Court Counsellors at the capital; where, the next year, he died. Most of his poetry was written during his Dazaifu years where he organized a circle of poets (including Yamanoue no Okura and Priest Manzei) anxious to demonstrate that, in literary prowess, their provincial centre at least equalled the standards of the capital. The *Manyoshu* contains more than 60 of his

poems in Japanese, all of which show an original and successful adaptation of Chinese literary ideas to a Japanese context; notable examples of which are his series of 13 *tanka* in praise of wine and drunkenness, a number of personal laments over the death of his wife in 728, and celebrations of plum-flowers written in the course of a poetry-party in the spring of 730. The *Kaifuso* (*Fond Recollections of Poetry*) of 751 includes an example of Tabito's poetry in Chinese. He himself appears to have been a highly intelligent, humane, and even easy-going man. Though steeped in Chinese culture, his poetry is firmly in the native Japanese tradition and is indeed a foundation-stone for the vast poetic structure subsequently erected by his eldest son, Yakamochi.

Takahashi no Mushimaro (early eighth century)
Very little is known of this poet except that he served as a provincial official under Fujiwara no Umakai (the governor of Hitachi province) in 712/713. Though he appears to have still been in government service as late as 723, his main poetic activity was probably during the earlier period in Hitachi where he was almost certainly concerned with the compilation of that province's official Topographical Record; and it is also likely that, together with other officials of that Eastern province, he had a hand in the revision of the *Azuma Uta* (*Eastern Songs*), provincial poetry of great importance (both for their poetic merit and for the dialect used) which became a striking contribution to the *Manyoshu*.

Priest Manzei (c.670–c.730)
While still a layman and known as Kasa no Maro, he rose to become Governor of Mino province in 706. His activity in organizing the building of the Kiso Highway was recognized in 714 by an increase in his pay. In 715 he also became governor of Owari province. In 719 he was made inspector-general over three provinces, and in 720

was promoted to an important post at Nara. In 721, possibly in order to qualify to offer prayers for the ailing forty-third Empress Gemmei, he became a monk and was subsequently a member of Otomo no Tabito's poetic circle (728–730) at Dazaifu where, from 723, he had been serving as Chief Commissioner for the construction of the Kwanzeon Temple.

Lady Kasa (–733)

She was probably a member of the same distinguished Kasa family as Priest Manzei, but our only knowledge of her is derived from the love poems associated with her love affair with Otomo no Yakamochi when he was a young courtier at Nara after his father Tabito returned there from Dazaifu in 730.

Yamabe no Akahito (–736)

He was essentially a court poet and, like Hitomaro, was relatively uninfluenced by the chinoiseries developed by the Dazaifu poetic circle. His particular strength was in writing about palaces and sacred landscapes which he visited in the train of the forty-fifth Emperor Shomu. Though renowned for his detailed observation of nature and his skill in composing *tanka*, his work was so traditional that, even to his young contemporary Otomo no Yakamochi, it already seemed old-fashioned. Nevertheless the later master-critic Ki no Tsurayuki in his introduction to the *First Imperial Anthology* of 905 pontificated that Akahito was as much a saint of poetry as Hitomaro, and that there was nothing to choose between them in the quality of their poetry.

Otomo no Sakanoue (699–781)

The date of this major poetess' birth is deduced from the fact that, as a young girl, a marriage was arranged in 714 between her and the elderly Prince Hozumi. In such upper-class marriages the bride was usually aged between 13 and 15. The Prince died in 715 and Sakanoue retired to her family's estate near Nara at Saho. Thereafter she married twice, but the order in which she married her two known husbands is not certain. It is most likely that her first husband (whom she married in 716) was her own elder half-brother Otomo no Sukunamaro by whom she had two daughters, the elder in 717 and the younger in 719. Such marriages between siblings born of necessarily different mothers was quite common as a means of cementing clan solidarity and may well be a surviving indicator of early Japanese matrilineal practices. Sukunamaro left the capital in 719 and is known to have been busy with audit-work in the provinces at least until 724 and to have died at some time between that date and 730. It is not known how this marriage broke down but at some point between 721 and 728 Sakanoue married Fujiwara no Maro who, born in 695, died of smallpox in 737. When Otomo no Tabito's wife died in Kyushu in 728, Sakanoue joined the gubernatorial household as her elder half-brother's hostess and managed that household until Tabito returned to Nara in 730. When Tabito died in 731, Sakanoue assumed leadership of the Otomo clan both as head priestess (*saidai miko*) and as clan matriarch (*toji*) in which capacities she supervised the upbringing (and poetic training) of Tabito's heir until Yakamochi came of age in 738 and, by then married to her elder daughter, finally took over as leader of the clan in 754. Sakanoue's last poem in the *Manyoshu* is addressed to her elder daughter when the latter set out in 750 to join her husband Yakamochi in Etchu where he had governed since 746. There are no further records of Sakanoue's subsequent life. However, it is recorded in a note to the *Shoku Nihongi* of 797 that in 781 Yakamochi was depressed by 'the recent death of his beloved mother'. Since his own mother had died in the Dazaifu in 728, this reference is almost certainly to the death of his maternal guardian, the Lady

Sakanoue. If therefore Sakanoue was still alive as a very old woman of 82 in 781, it is reasonable to ask what has become of the poetry which such a major poetess must have written during the last three decades of her life. There is no answer to such a question but, since the Otomo clan fell into virtually complete disgrace by their complicity in a failed plot of 785, it is at least possible that Sakanoue's later poetry appears as some of those anonymous poems of a recognizibly Manyoshu-style which are included in the *Kokinshu* (the *First Imperial Anthology*) compiled by Ki no Tsurayuki in 905. Sakanoue was the last great *Manyoshu* poet of the classical style, preserving all the classical verse-forms and technical devices and, though clearly the main influence on her innovative young nephew Yakamochi, herself writing mainly in the tradition of Hitomaro. The *Manyoshu* contains 77 of her *tanka*, six of her *choka* and one *sedoka*. Her particular genius was that she was able to employ conventional forms and all conventional poetic devices to express her own essentially personal feelings. She is in fact the greatest woman poet in the whole *Manyoshu*.

Otomo no Yotsuna (fl.c.730)
Practically nothing is known of this member of the Otomo clan except that he served under the clan head Tabito in the Dazaifu administration in an office concerned with the affairs of the frontier guards.

Lady Ki no Washika (c.700–   )
Was the daughter of a court official (Ki no Kahito) and married Prince Aki (fl.c.730) who was a great-grandson of the thirty-eighth Emperor Tenchi. The Prince's early love for his wife is expressed in 'Wave Crests', a *tanka* written when he was part of the Imperial train on a visit to Ise:

I would that they were flowers,
Those wave crests out in the bay,
That I might pick from the offing,
Pick and then carry away
To my wife at home their brief sea-blooms
In one vast white bouquet.

During the late 730s and early 740s she exchanged flirtatious poems with the young Otomo no Yakamochi, but they are more expressions of technical skill and court sophistication than of genuine passion. There are no reliable records of her later life.

Lady Nakatomi (fl.c.740)
Nothing is known of this Lady but, from her five poems addressed to Otomo no Yakamochi, it can be assumed that she was another of the court ladies with whom he was connected as a young courtier.

Mother of a Mission Member (fl.c.733)
Nothing is known of this poetess except the poem she wrote on the occasion when her son left Naniwa (now Osaka) by ship in 733, as a member of a diplomatic mission to China.

Ki no Toyokawa (fl.c.739)
The *Manyoshu* contains only one poem by this member of the prestigious Ki clan, of whom nothing is known except that he was promoted to the fifth court rank in 739.

Sanu Chigami (fl.c.738)
Was a relatively low-ranked attendant at the Great Shrine of Ise, an occupation which required no communication whatever with men. Her love poems exchanged with, and marriage to (c.738), Nakatomi Yakamori led to his dismissal from court and dispatch in disgrace to Echizen. He was not included in the general amnesty

of 748, but was later pardoned and is known to have been back at court in 763. Nothing more is known of Sanu Chigami.

Tanabe no Fukumaro (fl.c.748)

He is known to have been a court officer in charge of wine in March 748; and later to have been sent on duty by Tachibana no Moroe (the Great Minister at Nara) to see Otomo no Yakamochi at his provincial headquarters in Etchu; where he attended a banquet given for him by the governor. He left a collection of poems, all now lost except for those included in the *Manyoshu*.

Lady Heguri (fl.c.750)

No information about this poetess survives, except for the twelve songs she sent to Otomo no Yakamochi after he left Nara to take up his governor's post in Etchu in 746. From these poems Lady Heguri can be assumed to have been another of those ladies with whom Yakamochi conducted a flirtation during his years as a young courtier in Nara.

Lady Hirokawa (fl.c.750)

Again, virtually nothing is known of this lady except that she was a grand-daughter of Prince Hozumi (the seventh son of the fortieth Emperor Temmu) and that in 763 she was promoted to the fifth court rank.

Hasetsukabe no Inamaro (fl.c.750)

Nothing is known of this conscript-soldier except that he was from Suruga.

Imamatsuribe no Yosafu (fl.c.750)

Again, nothing is known of this conscript-soldier except that he was from Shimousa and in charge of ten men.

Princess Yashiro (fl.c.755)

Virtually nothing is known of this Princess apart from a reference in the *Shoku Nihongi* (*Continuation of the Chronicles of Japan: 697–791*) of 797 to a scandalous Imperial liaison, which presumably underlies the poem 'Shame'. It is also recorded that at the time of the abdication of the forty-fifth Emperor Shomu in 758, she was appointed to the fourth court rank.

Otomo no Miyori (–774)

In 730 he was a governor of Bungo under the overall administration of Otomo no Tabito in the Dazaifu. In 748 he was promoted to the fifth court rank and became vice-minister for justice, in which capacity he was in charge of the central office for tax collection. He was thereafter made governor of several provinces of middling importance, and had reached the fourth court rank by the time of his death.

Otomo no Yakamochi (718–785)

Was the main, if not the only, compiler of the *Manyoshu* whose 4516 poems include 473 of his own. The Otomo (Great Escort) were an ancient and major military clan whose founder was held to have distinguished himself as a military leader in the service of Ninigi, that mythological offspring of deities who was sent down from heaven to rule Japan. Early Japanese history includes many famous members of the clan who were generals and similarly important government officers, notably that Otomo who, on behalf of the 1st Emperor Jimmu (allegedly 711–585BC) fought across southern Japan from Kyushu to the Kyoto-Osaka heartland of the eventual state of Yamato, and was granted the unusually honorific title of Michi no Omi (Retainer of the Way). The later history of the clan includes other notably warlike but reliable retainers, characteristics which earned them the hereditary command of the

Imperial Guards who were all sons of great families. The clan's power was at its greatest during the fifth and sixth centuries but, at the time of the *Manyoshu*, was already deeply on the wane as the warrior qualities which characterized them became less important to the Yamato State than the bureaucratic skills of other clans. Yakamochi's father Tabito was less successful than his predecessors, and only rose to prominence comparatively late in life with his appointment to command at Dazaifu in 725/6. Yakamochi spent five or six boyhood years in Kyushu with his father until Tabito, in 730, returned to Nara on promotion. Tabito died in 731 and Yakamochi, then barely 14, continued his education under private tutors on the family estate at Saho just outside Nara until, in 737 or 738, he joined the Imperial bodyguard and became an Imperial attendant at court. This was a largely decorative function and Yakamochi appears to have spent his time in chasing women and polishing his skills as a poet. His first real love (whose name is not known) died in 739 leaving a small son. Later that year Yakamochi began a serious courtship of the elder daughter of his aunt, the Lady Sakanoue. Throughout these years political turmoil was on the brew and became so open a revolt in 740 that the forty-fifth Emperor Shomu fled the capital to establish his court at Kuni. The revolt was eventually put down, but Prince Asaka (the then Crown Prince to whom the Otomo were closely linked) died of Fujiwara poison in 744. Yakamochi continued to serve in the court train but with no specific occupation (probably because he was working for the Great Minister Tachibana no Moroe on collecting material for the *Manyoshu*) until he was appointed an assistant minister of the Imperial household in April 746 and shortly thereafter, in July 746, to be governor of the important province of Etchu. He remained in that post until 751 when he returned to Nara as a Middle Counsellor (*Shonagon*). When the Emperor Shomu, a weak ruler mainly concerned with propagating Buddhism, abdicated in 757, his daughter by a Fujiwara woman became the Empress Koken. This Empress was dominated by her lover and political adviser Fujiwara no Nakamaro with a consequent decline in the power of Tachibana no Moroe and his supporters. Yakamochi nevertheless continued from 751–754 as a member of Moroe's Great Council of State, becoming a junior assistant minister of war under Moroe's son. In this capacity he was concerned with drafting frontier-guards and thus easily able to collect, in 755, those poems by frontier-guards which are included in the *Manyoshu*. In 755 the now-retired Emperor Shomu fell sick and lost all influence on the conduct of affairs. Moroe was in fact obliged to resign in disgrace. The retired Emperor died in 756 and the Empress Koken and her Fujiwara lover began actively to attack all Otomo clan-members. Though Yakamochi tried to keep out of trouble, his position became even worse when Moroe died in 757; at which time Moroe's son and many of Yakamochi's Otomo cousins became involved in unsuccessful plots and finally a rebellion which led to their execution. Yakamochi was not involved, but lost his position in the ministry of war, retaining only a minor post on the Great Council of State. In 758 he was appointed to the unimportant province of Inaba where he wrote for his officers' New Year party of 759 the latest-dated poem in the whole *Manyoshu* [not included in this collection]. In 762 he returned to Nara as a senior assistant Minister of Central Affairs, but was sufficiently involved in the next failed plot against the Empress and her Fujiwara advisers to be sent off in 764 to be governor of another unimportant province, Satsuma. He thereafter served in a variety of other insignificant posts until the Empress died in 770, and Yakamochi was then re-appointed to the Great Council though still at a fairly junior level. In 771 his fortunes took a turn for the better when he was granted junior fourth court rank and for the next ten years fared reasonably well. In 781 he was appointed master of the household of the Crown Prince and promoted to junior third rank,

but was forced to resign in 782 by reason of involvement in yet
another court intrigue. Within six months he was restored to his
mastership and was also made a General. This last appointment was
as Commander in Chief of the Eastern Expeditionary Force (*sei–tai–
shogun*: Barbarian-Quelling Generalissimo) concerned with 'peace-
keeping against the Ainu', and is probably the first use of the
Shogun title which, from the thirteenth to nineteenth centuries was
used to describe the feudal military dictators who effectively ruled
Japan. In 783 he became a Middle Counsellor on the Great Council
and remained in that relatively influential position until his death in
785. However, within a few days of his death two of his close rela-
tives were involved in an assassination attempt in support of the
Crown Prince. The attempt failed, the Crown Prince was banished
and starved to death and the whole Otomo family was stripped of
its property and positions. Yakamochi's remains were exhumed,
unranked and, together with his son, banished. This injustice was
eventually recognized, and in 806 his remains were regranted his
junior third court rank and returned to Nara. Yakomochi is not
only important for his work as a compiler but because his own
poems in the *Manyoshu* (426 *tanka*, 46 *choka* and one *sedoka*) repre-
sent the development of Japanese poetry from the robust early
tradition of communal writings (he was always extremely con-
scious of his traditional family status) to individual sensitivity. He
is celebrated for his fore-shadowing of later Heian poetic feeling
and, in contemporary Japan, for the peculiar modernity of his so-
called 'spring sadness'. No Yakamochi poem later than 759 is
known to exist but, as in the case of the Lady Sakanoue, it is at least
possible that some of the anonymous poems in the *First Imperial
Anthology* (the *Kokinshu* of 905) are from his hand.